THE
NEW YORKER

BOOK OF MOM CARTOONS

The New Yorker Book of Mom Cartoons copyright © 2008 by *The New Yorker Magazine*.
All rights reserved. Printed in the United States of America. For permission information, write
Andrews McMeel Publishing, LLC, 4520 Main St., Kansas City, Missouri 64111.

08 09 10 11 12 BBG 10 9 8 7 6 5 4 3 2 1

ISBN-13: 978-0-7407-7603-8
ISBN-10: 0-7407-7603-7

Library of Congress Control Number: 2007942376

www.andrewsmcmeel.com

ATTENTION: SCHOOLS AND BUSINESSES

Andrews McMeel books are available at quantity discounts with bulk purchase for educational,
business, or sales promotional use. For information, please write to: Special Sales Department,
Andrews McMeel Publishing, LLC, 4520 Main Street, Kansas City, Missouri 64111.

THE
NEW YORKER

BOOK OF MOM CARTOONS

**Andrews McMeel
Publishing, LLC**
Kansas City

THE
NEW YORKER

BOOK OF MOM CARTOONS

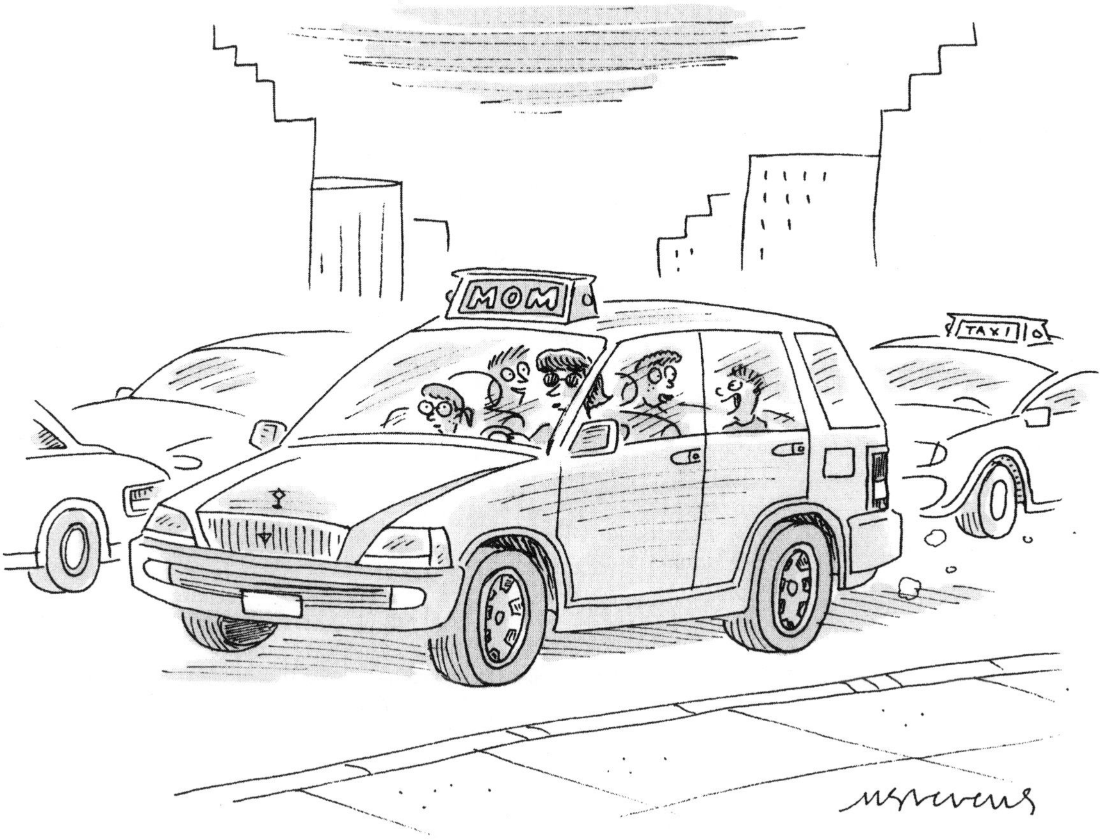
MOM
TAXI

"If your mother asks, we crossed at the corner."

"My mother doesn't even bother to come to the games."

"Son, your mother is a remarkable woman."

MOM-O-GRAMS
"You look too thin,
Your face is pale.
This is the path
That leads to jail."
"Ask anyone who knows
about science:
You don't use wet hands
to unplug an
appliance."
"You live in a hovel,
It's really quite bleak.
You might try to vacuum
At least once a week."
R. Chast

"It's six o'clock, Family Network time. And now, here's Mom with the news."

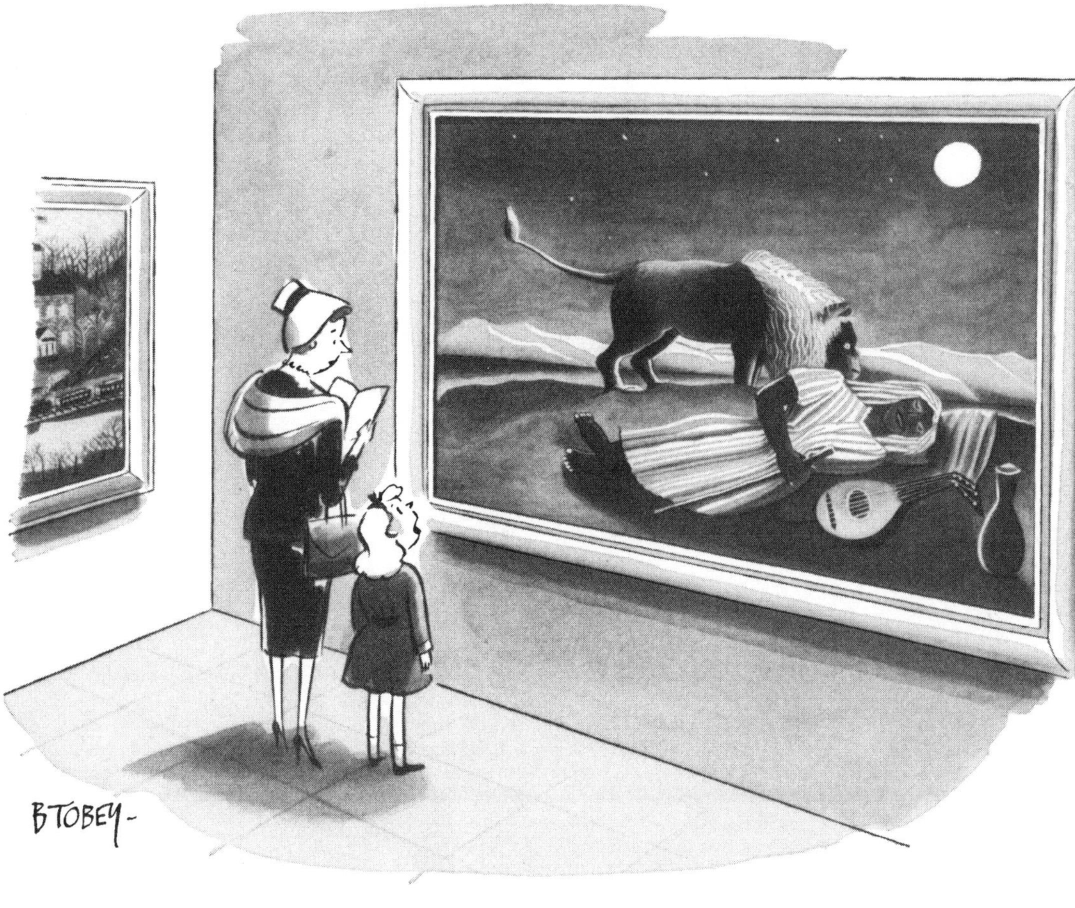
B TOBEY

"Then what happened?"

"If you promise to be very careful, Mommy will let you carry the baguettes."

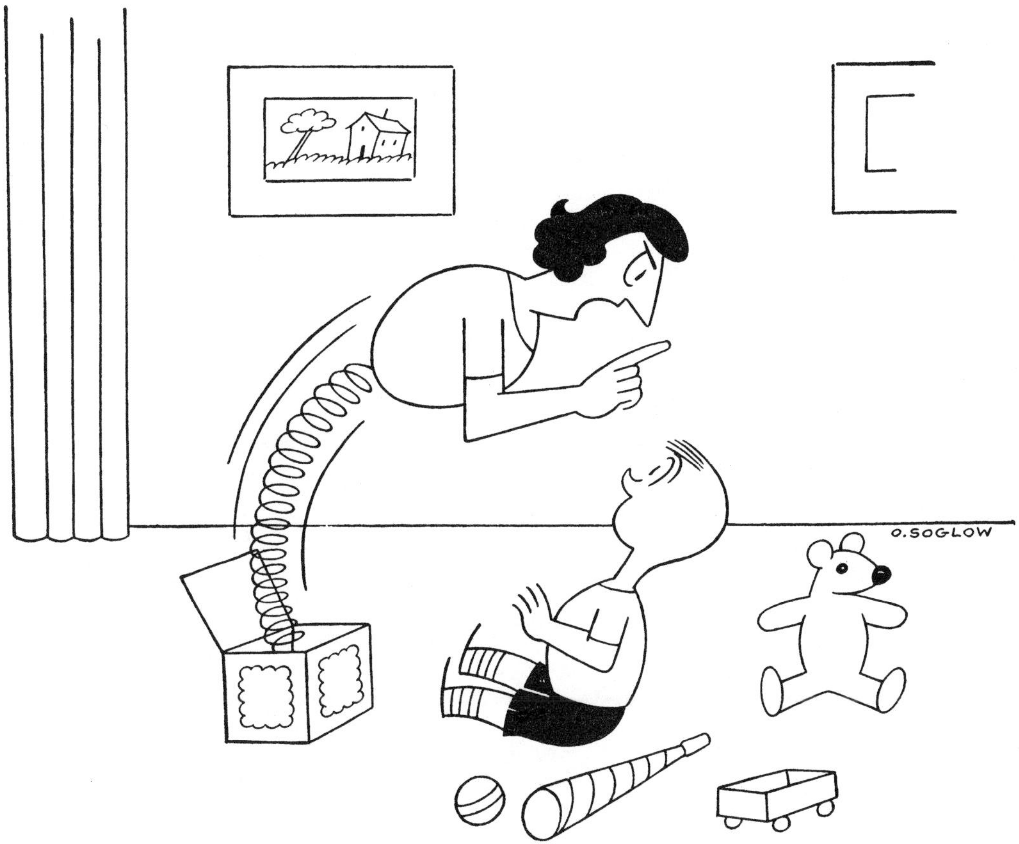
O. SOGLOW

"Today the secret ingredients for Mom's Apple Pie were sold
to the Japanese for sixty-eight million dollars."

*"What would you suggest that would make
a nine-year-old boy's mother happy?"*

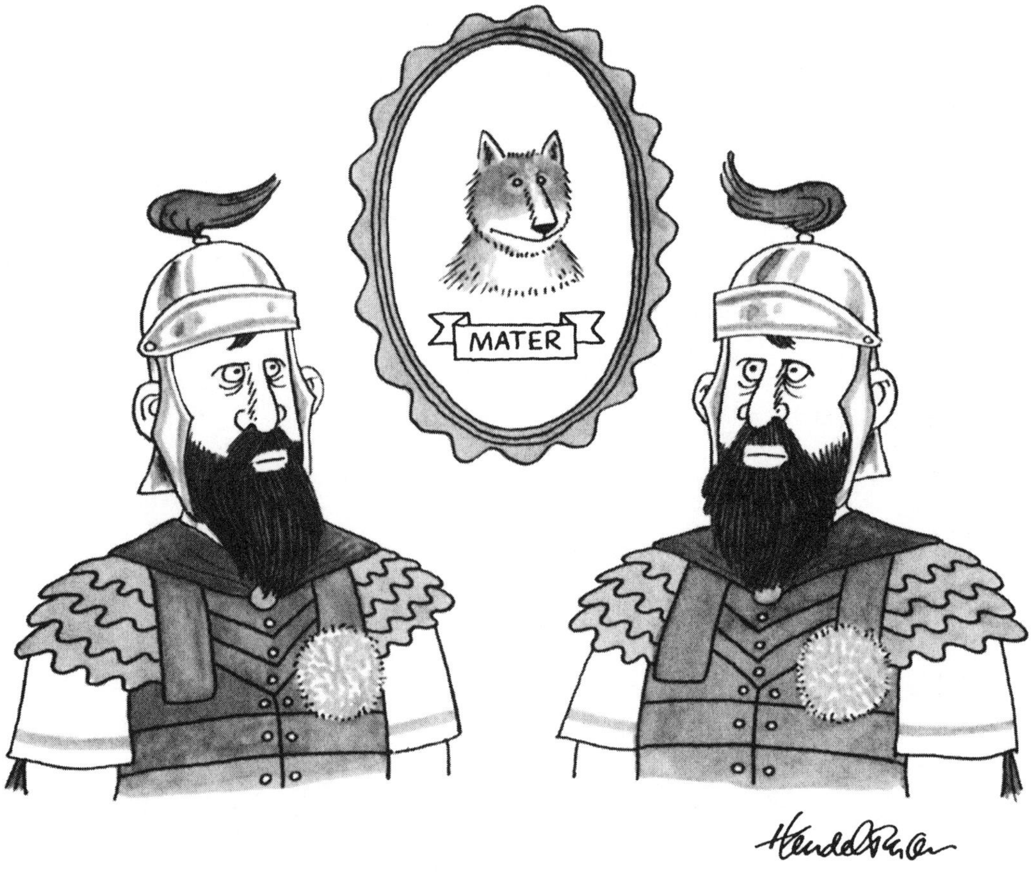
MATER

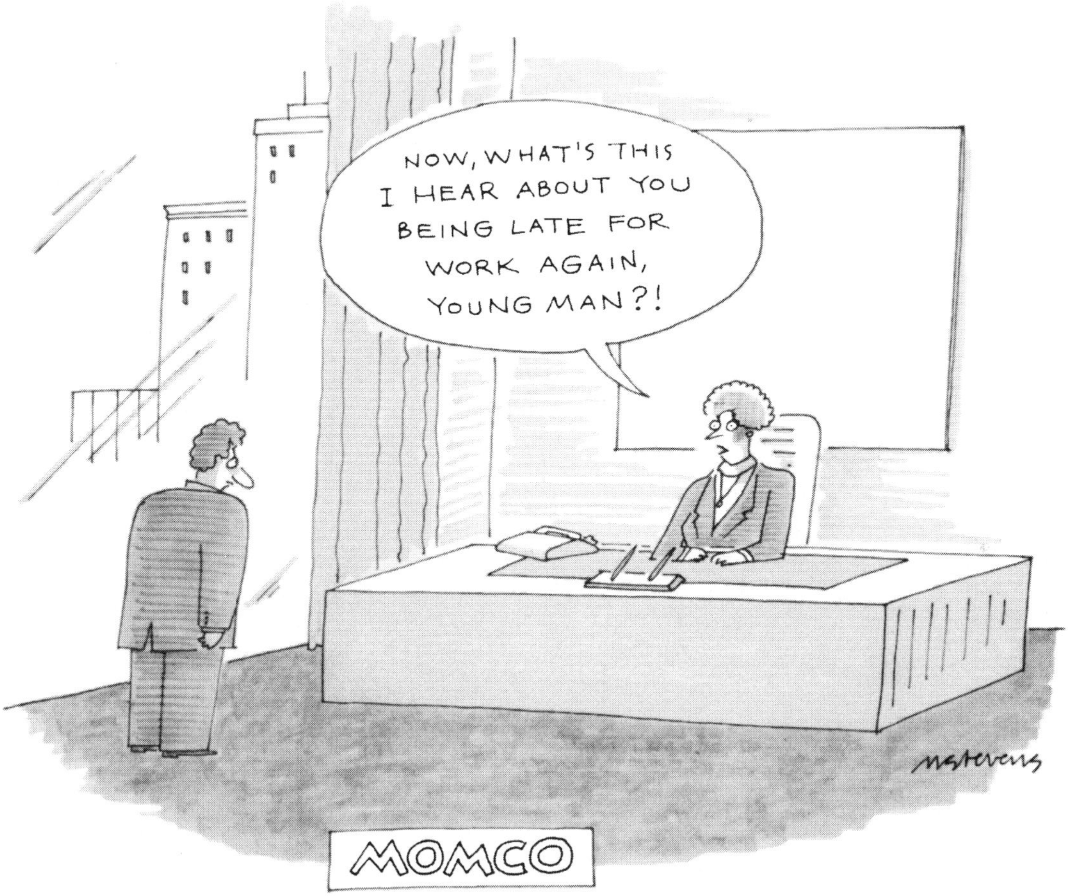
NOW, WHAT'S THIS I HEAR ABOUT YOU BEING LATE FOR WORK AGAIN, YOUNG MAN?!
MOMCO
mstevens

"I'm making a scrapbook to document the most embarrassing moments of your life."

"Zebra to Cobra—for the last time, your lunch is getting cold. Over and out."

"*Brad? This is your congressman. Get Mommy on the phone, please.*"

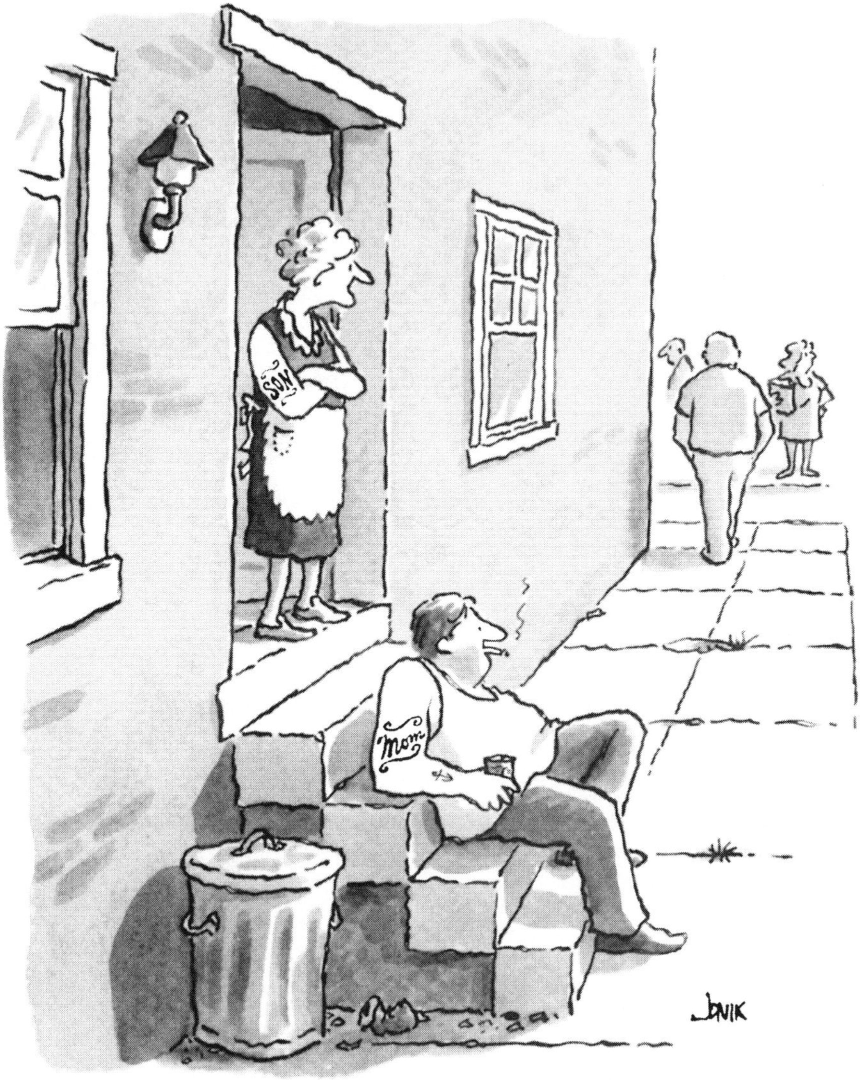
SON
Mom
JONIK

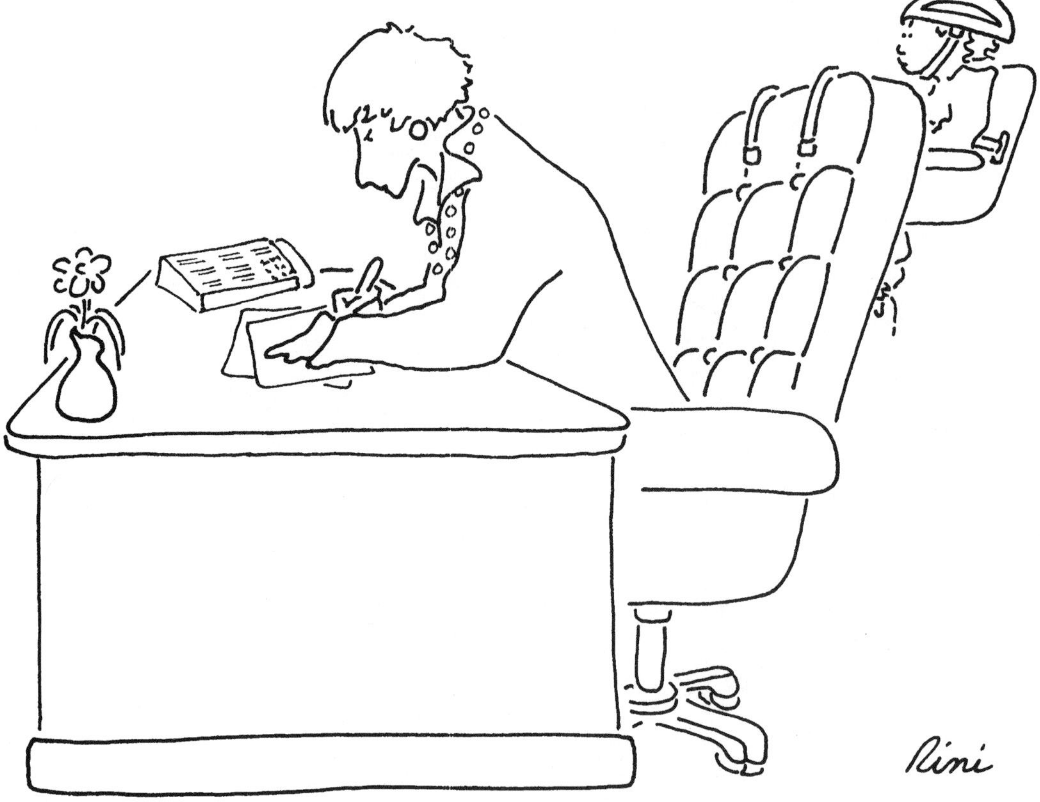
Rini

"Well, that should keep your mother quiet for a while."

"My mother could cook rings around your mother."

"Mom, are we waterproof or just water-resistant?"

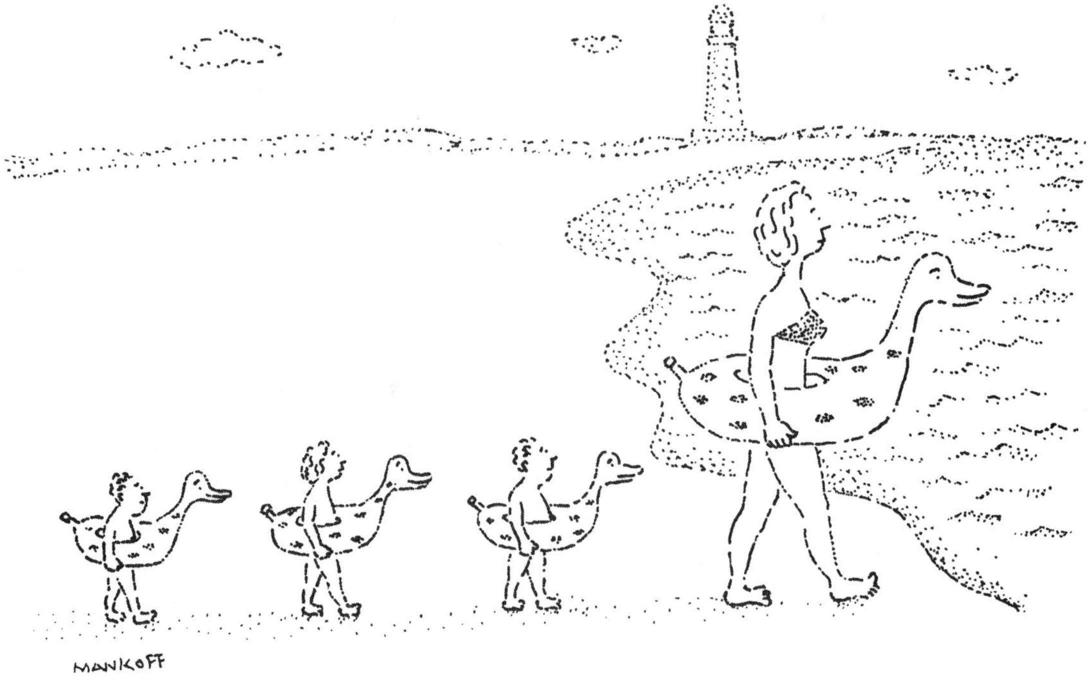
MANKOFF

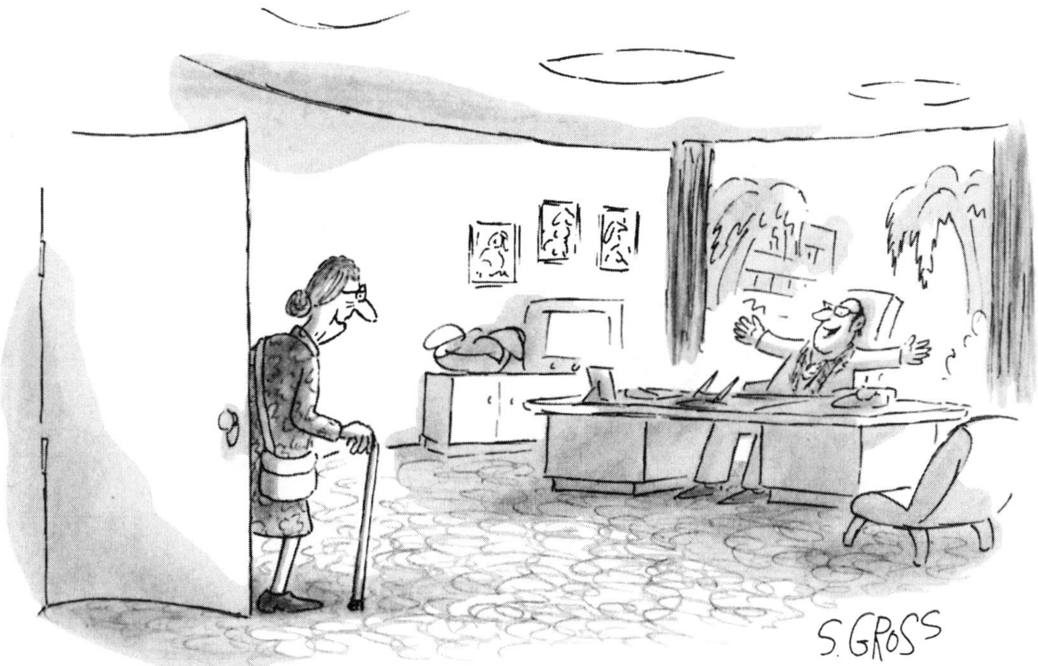
S. GROSS

"Mom baby!"

"*Really, Mother, I don't need any help!*"

"All rise."

Mother Goose and Mother Nature
Play Canasta

"Thank you all for coming. Starting next year, Mother's Days will find me at the Desert Palm Spa."

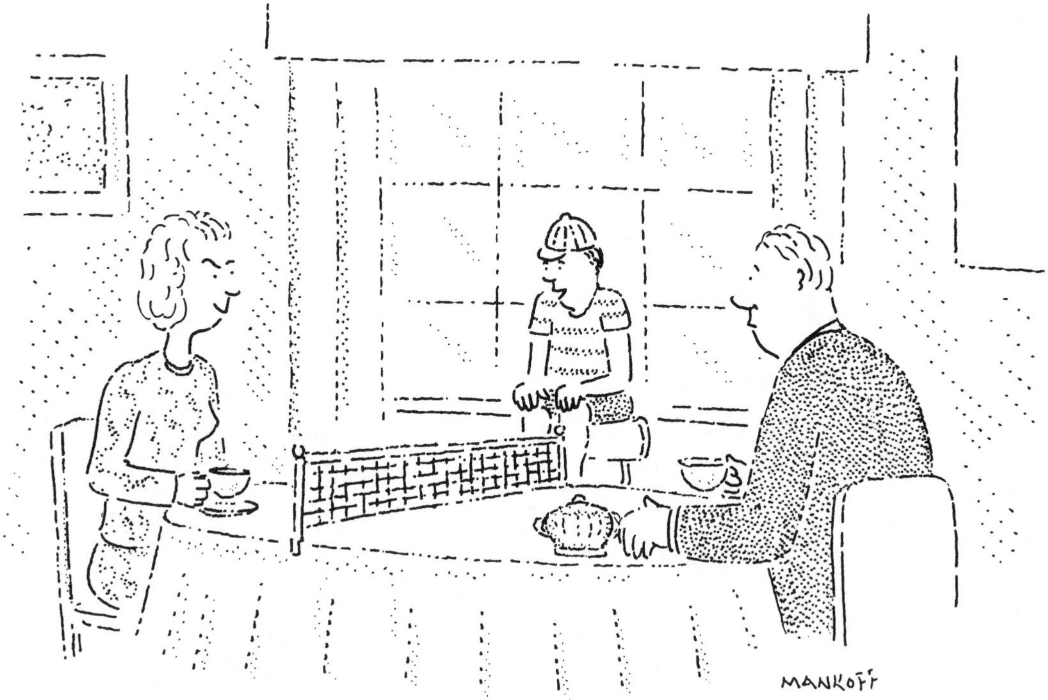
MANKOFF

"Advantage, Mom."

"*Career track or mommy track?*"

"Mommy says she's lived in a cage without bars for years."

"You ungrateful little beast! How dare you accuse me of being an overbearing stage mother! Go to your room and stay there!"

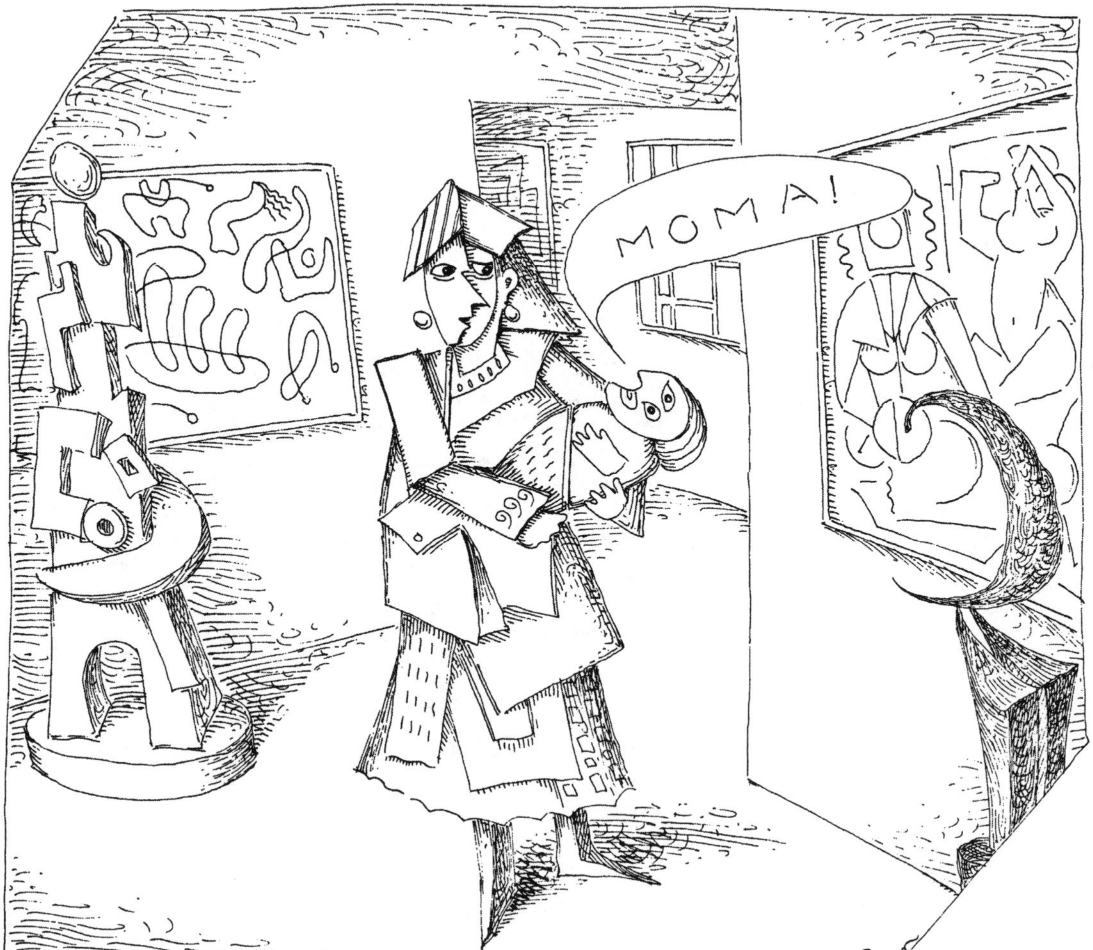
MOMA!
John O'Brien

EVE'S MOM

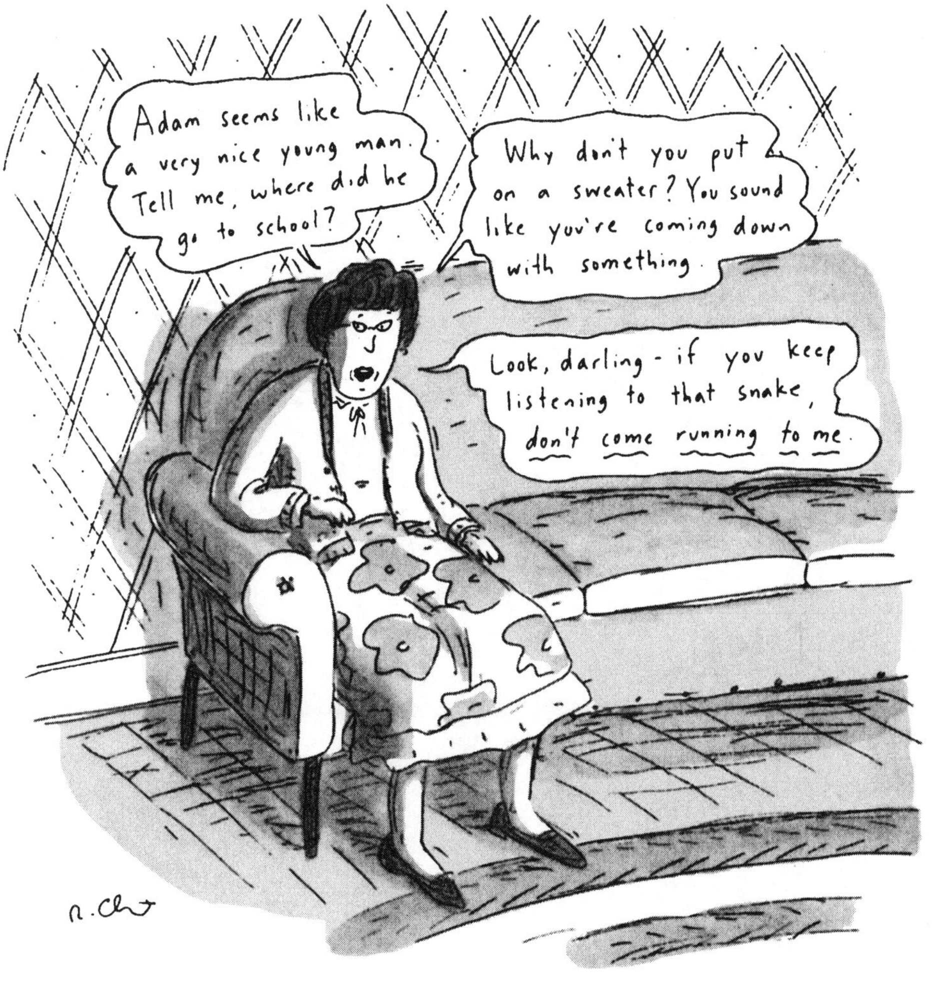
Adam seems like a very nice young man. Tell me, where did he go to school?
Why don't you put on a sweater? You sound like you're coming down with something.
Look, darling - if you keep listening to that snake, don't come running to me.
R. Cht

"Your mommy, Caitlin, is a hired gun."

"Mom, Dad—I'm adopted, aren't I?"

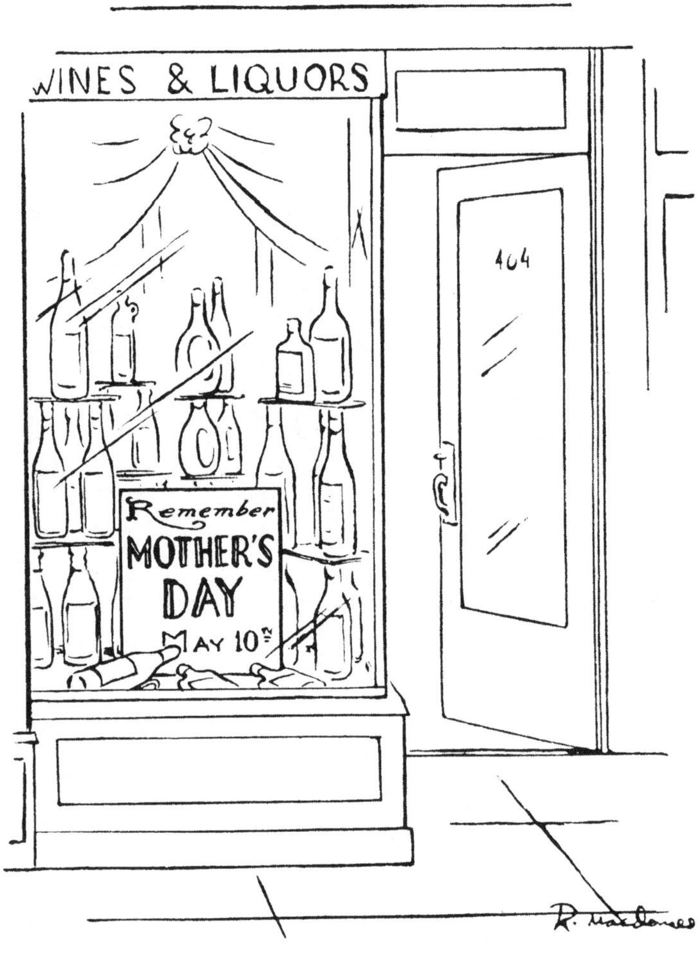
WINES & LIQUORS
404
Remember
MOTHER'S
DAY
MAY 10TH

"Now can we have an eating experience?"

"*For heaven's sake, Melissa, she's my mother. I can't tell her to leave.*"

"Dad, if Mom ever has a boyfriend, I hope he's just like you."

"Whenever Mother's Day rolls around, I regret having eaten my young."

B. Smaller

"They're not dingy, Mother, they're unbleached."

"Damn it, agree to whatever she demands.
No matter what it takes, I want my mommy."

"My mother doesn't understand me."

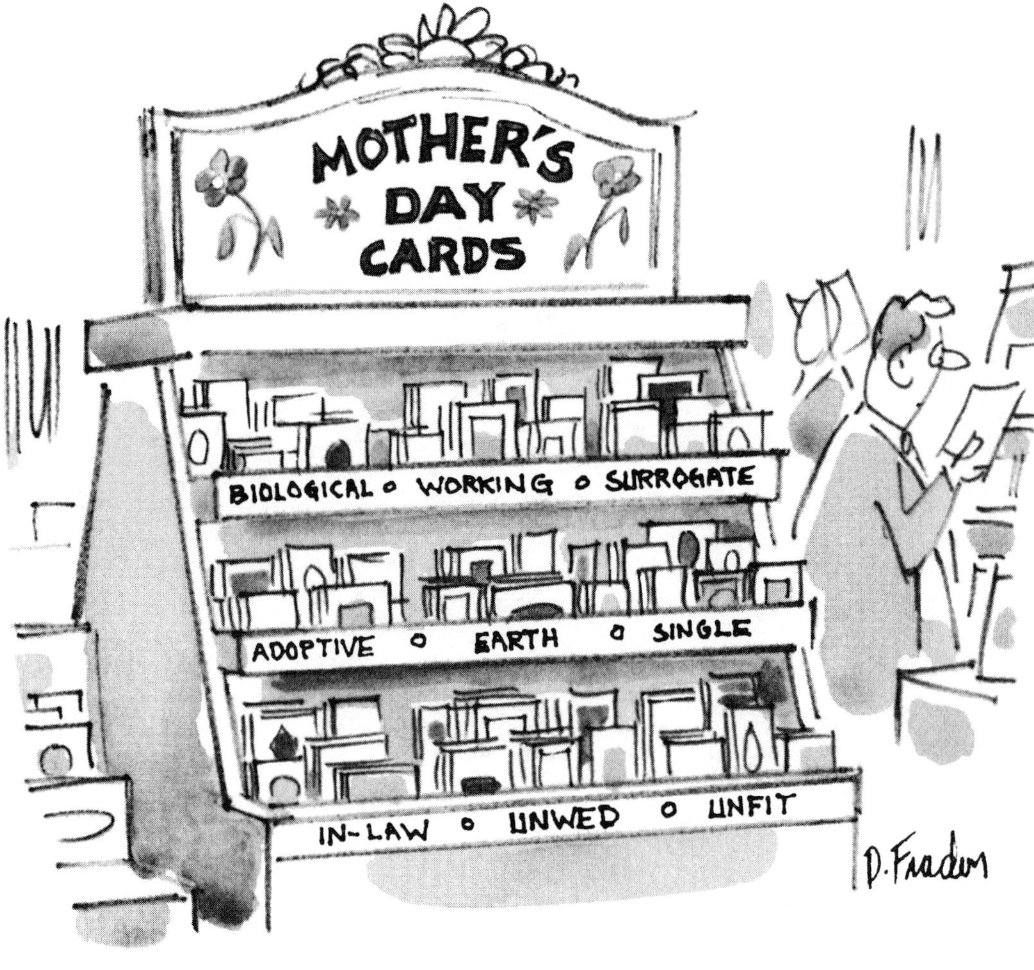
MOTHER'S DAY CARDS
BIOLOGICAL o WORKING o SURROGATE
ADOPTIVE o EARTH o SINGLE
IN-LAW o UNWED o UNFIT
D. Fradon

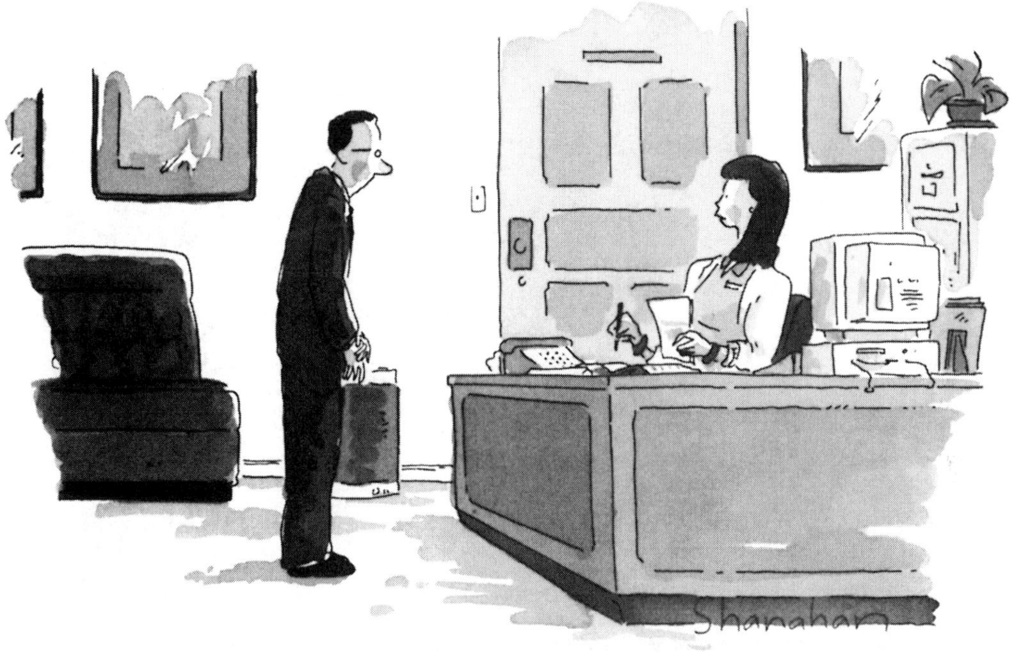
Shanahan

"You're at the top of the list, Mr. Stewart, and you'll be immediately notified the moment there's an available womb for you to crawl back into."

"Some kids at school called you a feminist, Mom, but I punched them out."

"Listen, Mom, I'm not your little girl anymore."

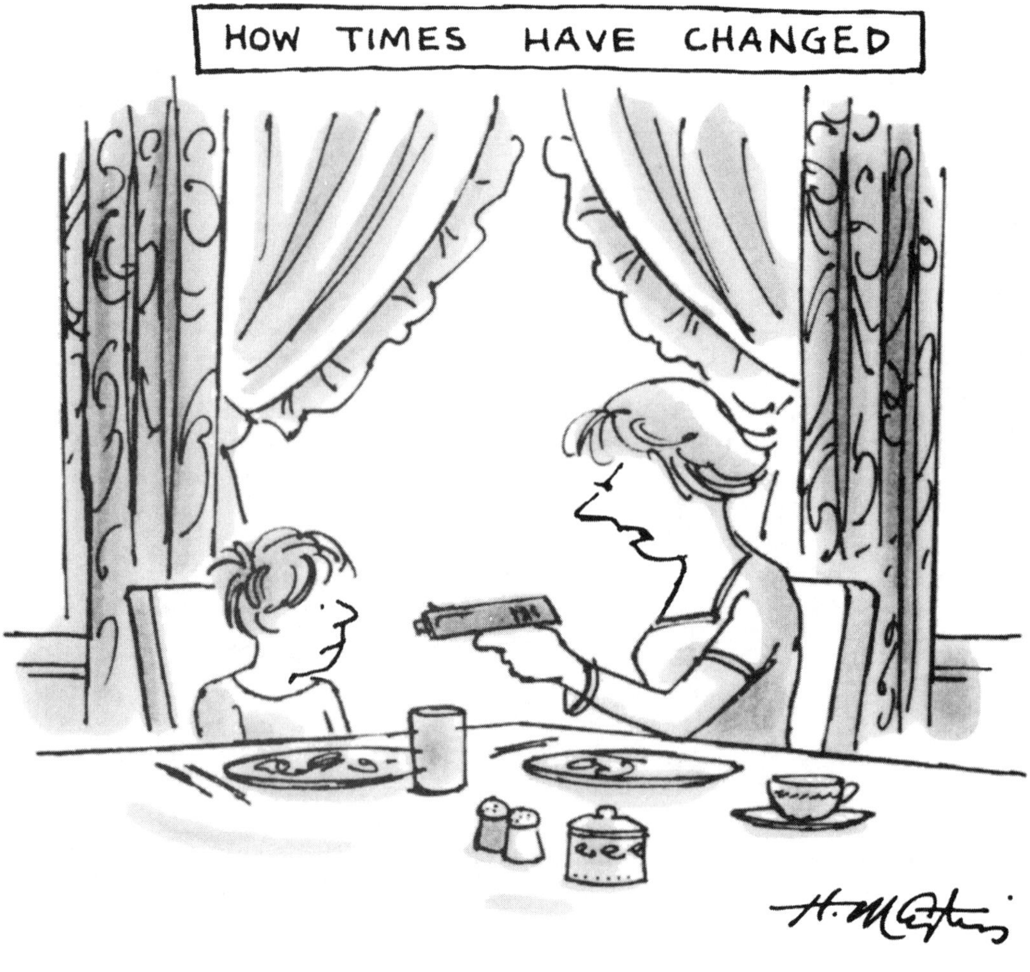
HOW TIMES HAVE CHANGED

"Eat your carrots!"

"To my favorite palindrome."

"She has her mother's management style."

"Do you have any cards for two mommies?"

B. Smaller

"Actually, I do look a lot like my mom. It's just that I have her first nose."

"You order for me, Mom. You know what I like."

JIMMY, SIXTH-GENERATION PAIN IN THE ASS

"Hey, look—Mom left us an internal memo."

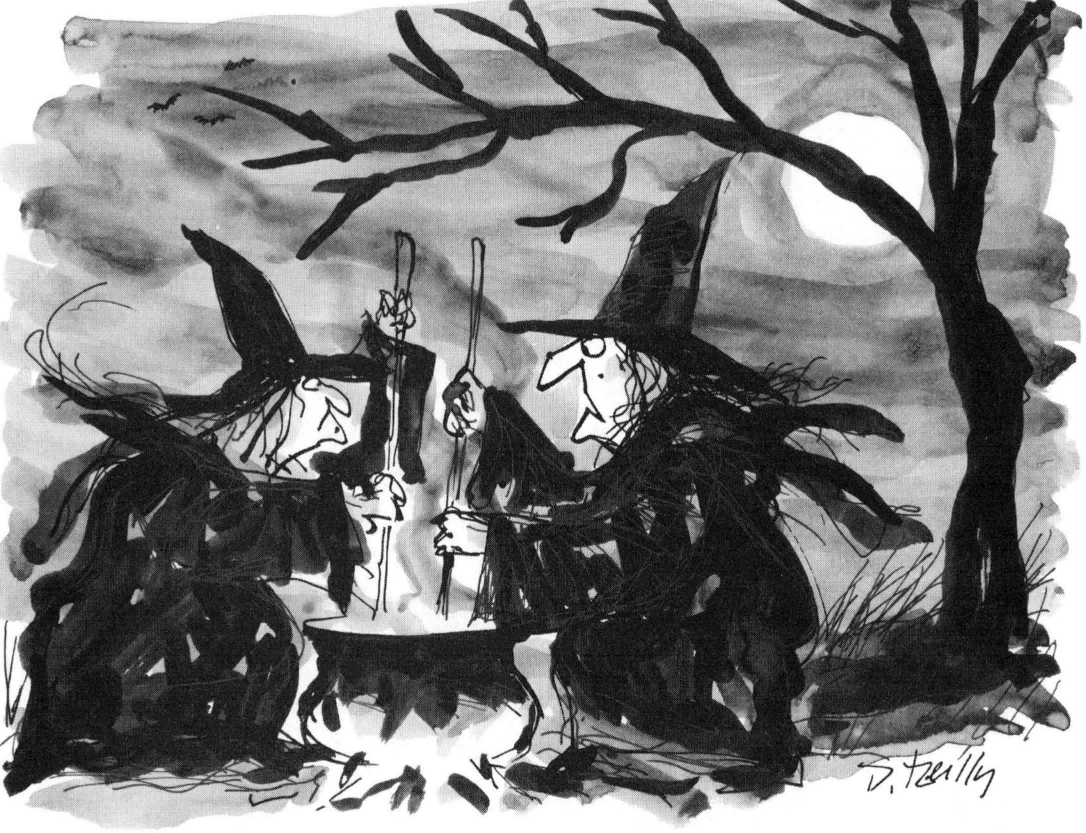
D. Reilly

"What I really hate is knowing that I'm doing this exactly the way my mother did it."

"I dislike you both the same."

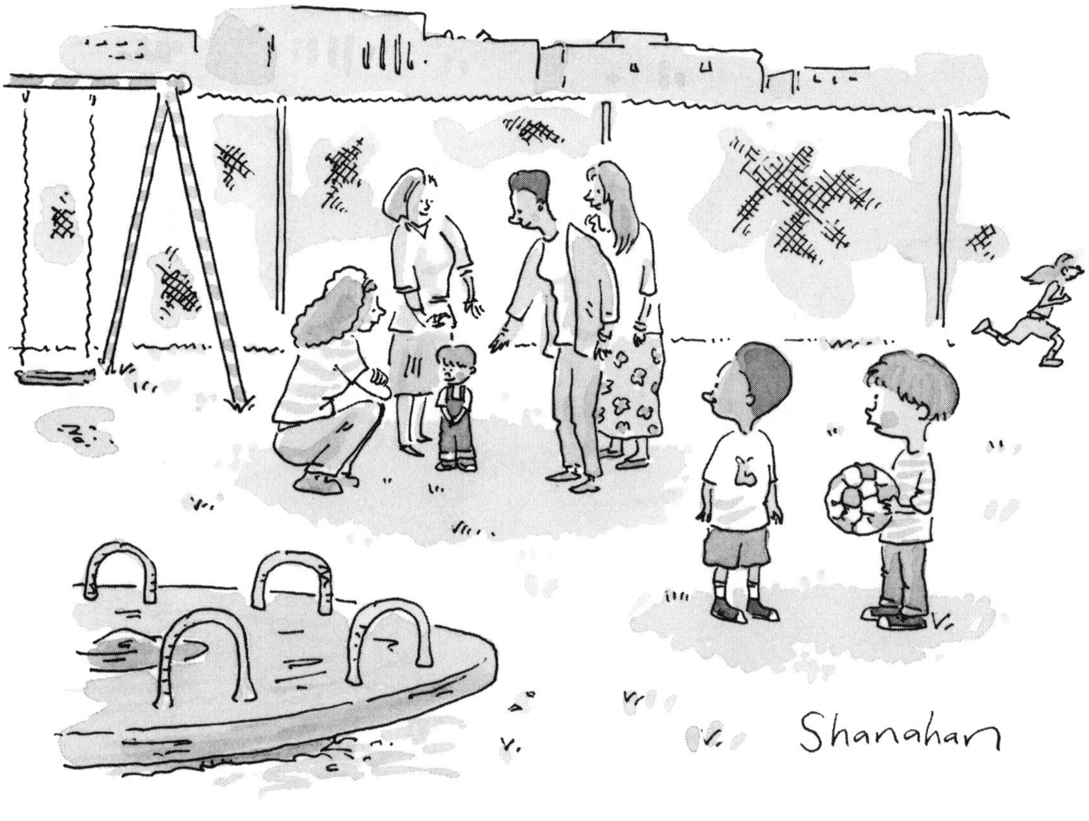
Shanahan

"He's a real mom magnet."

"That's nothing. My mom is older than the Super Bowl."

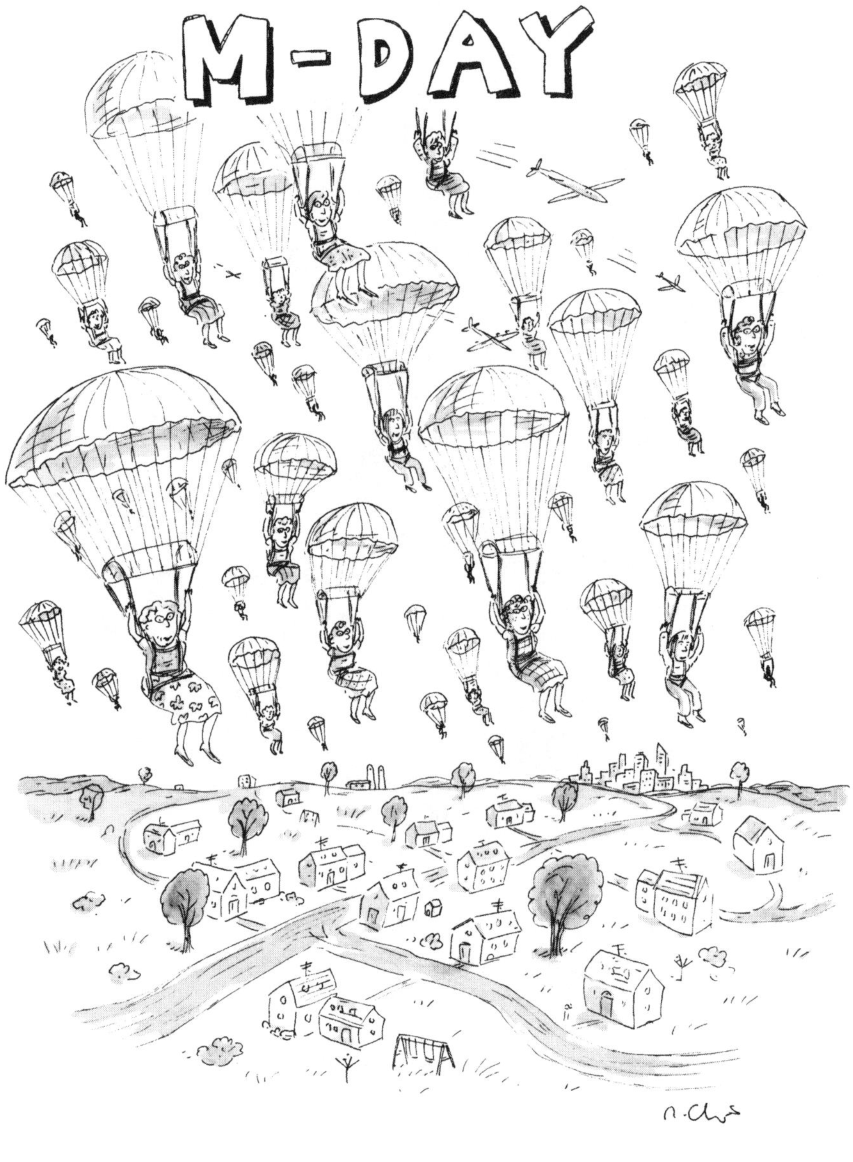
M-DAY

"Don't you dare put Mommy on hold again."

"He's just doing that to get attention."

"Nice try, Mom, but I'm going to go with a caterer."

"Mommy, Becky says she's not going to put me in her memoirs!"

"If Mom catches us out here, we're really gonna get it!"

"What did I tell you about destroying Mommy's inner balance?"

THE SURRENDERED MOM

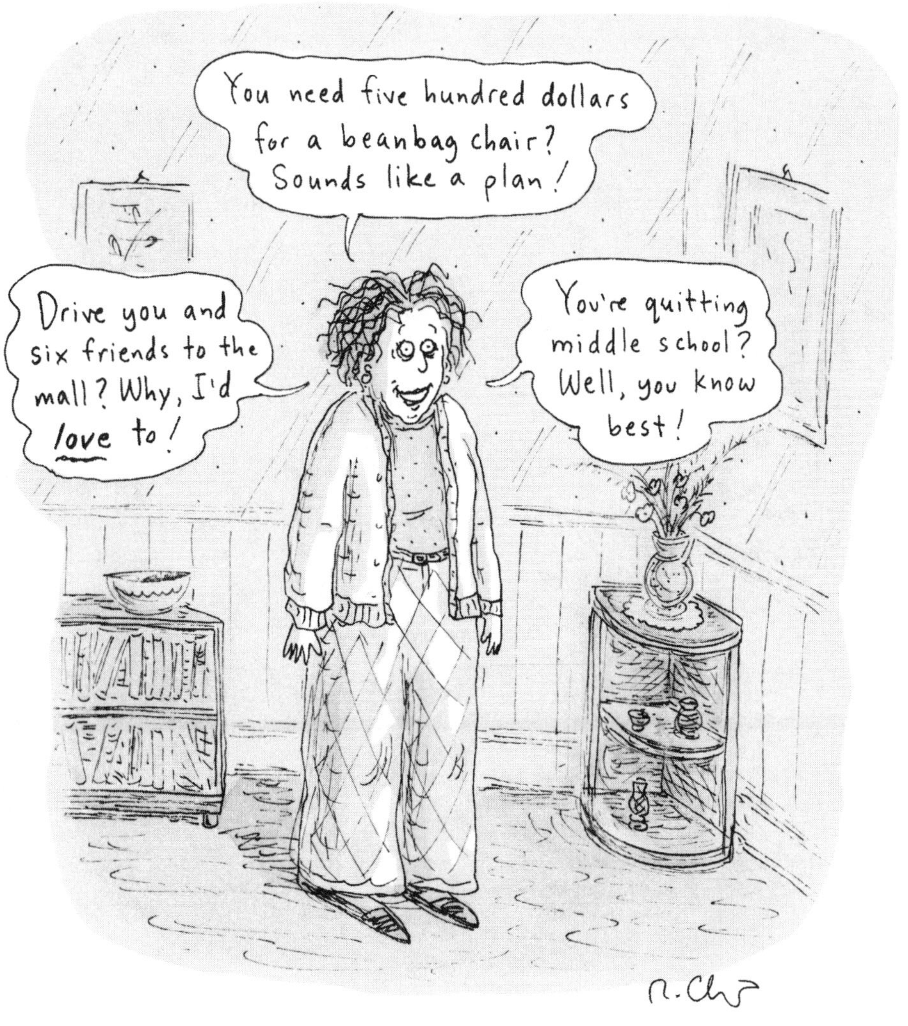
You need five hundred dollars for a beanbag chair? Sounds like a plan!
Drive you and six friends to the mall? Why, I'd love to!
You're quitting middle school? Well, you know best!
R. Chast

"I think Dad is the reason Mom never married."

"I never had to choose between a baby and a career—I'm a surrogate mother."

"Why are you special? Because I'm your mommy, and I'm special."

"My gosh! You remind me so much of your father when he was in prison."

"Your mother was in here looking for you."

"You still keep all the old pictures on display, don't you, Mama."

"Will you turn that TV down? Can't you see I'm on the phone?"

"*They got extinct because they didn't listen to their mommies.*"

"Don't forget to click Reply."

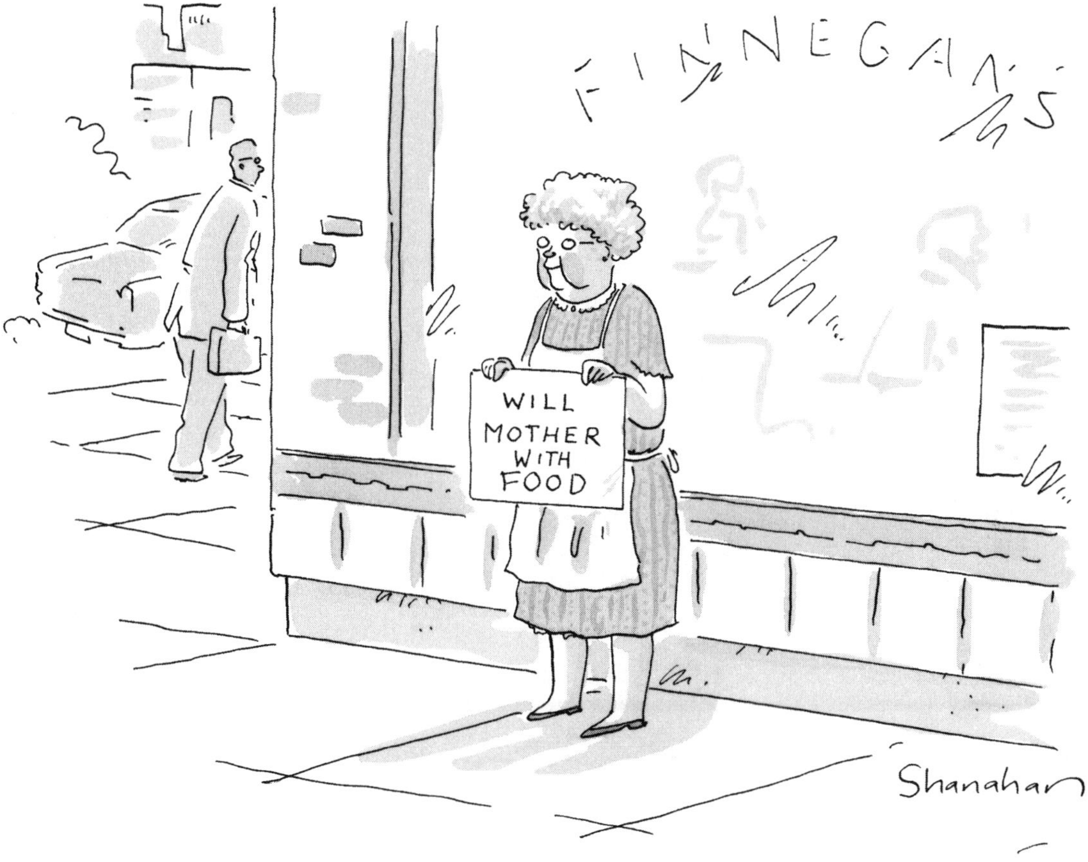
FINNEGAN'S
WILL
MOTHER
WITH
FOOD
Shanahan

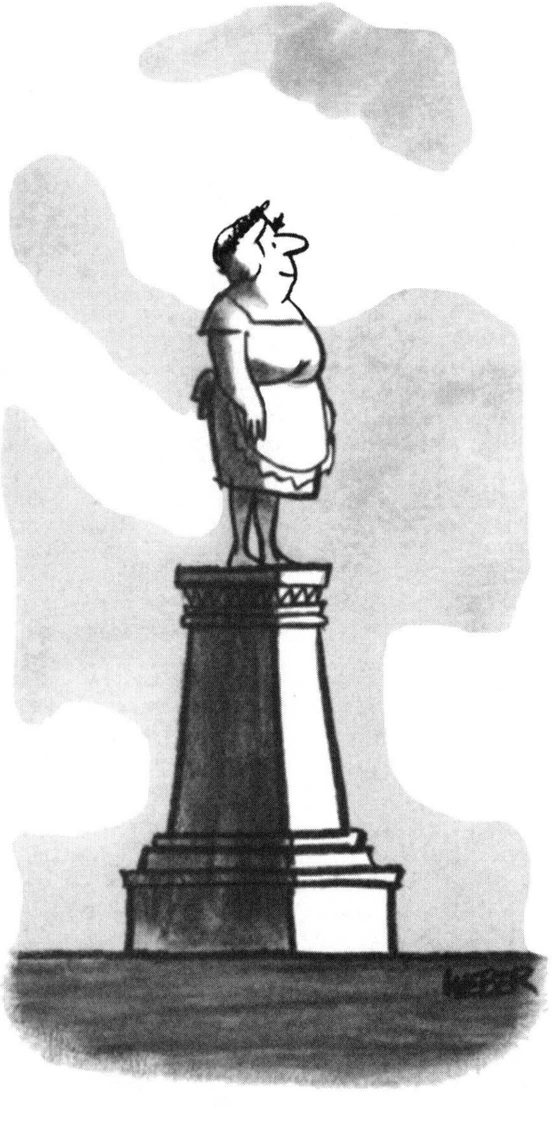
WEBER

"Mommy usually reads me a story, then slips me a twenty."

"What should we attach shame to today?"

"Oh, Christ—it's your mother."

"She'll buy it for us. We just have to stay on message."

"You'd tell me if I was genetically modified?"

"Don't forget Mommy's yoga mat, Simon!"

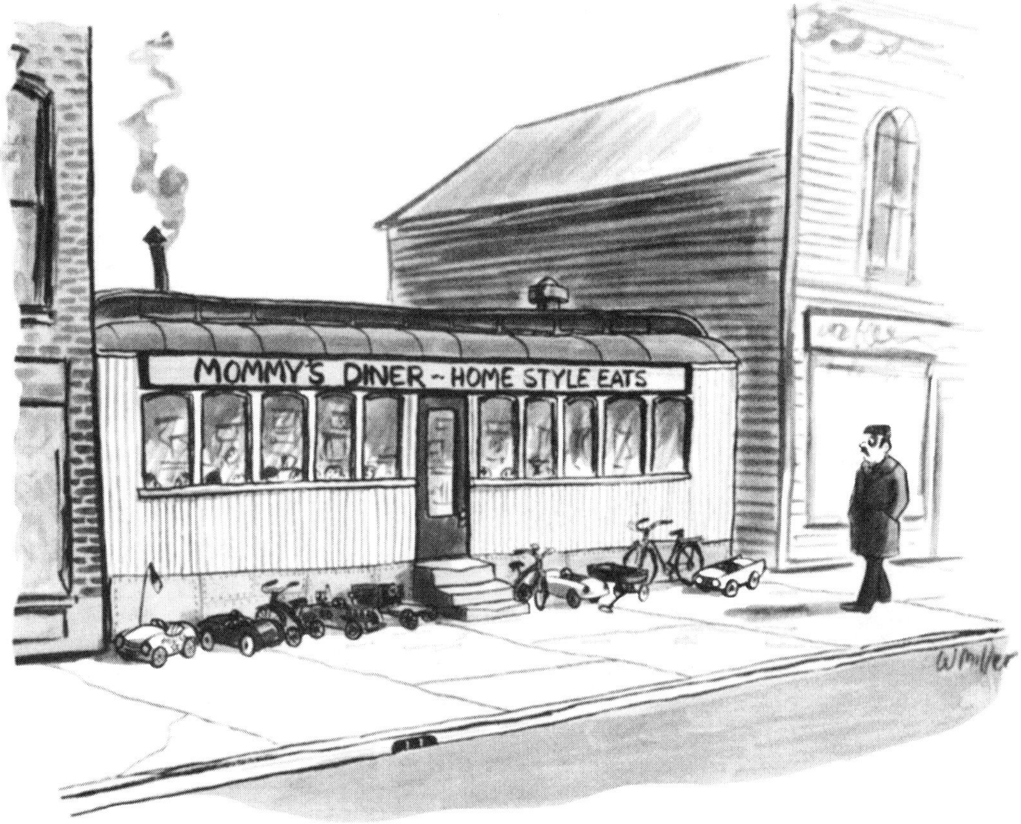
MOMMY'S DINER ~ HOME STYLE EATS
WMiller

"It's O.K., kids—your mother's just having an argument."

"Alternatively, your mother could have a cooking disorder."

"We've been over this before—you're too young to feel emasculated."

"My relationship with my mother has really improved thanks to Caller I.D."

"You're why I have the moat, Mother."

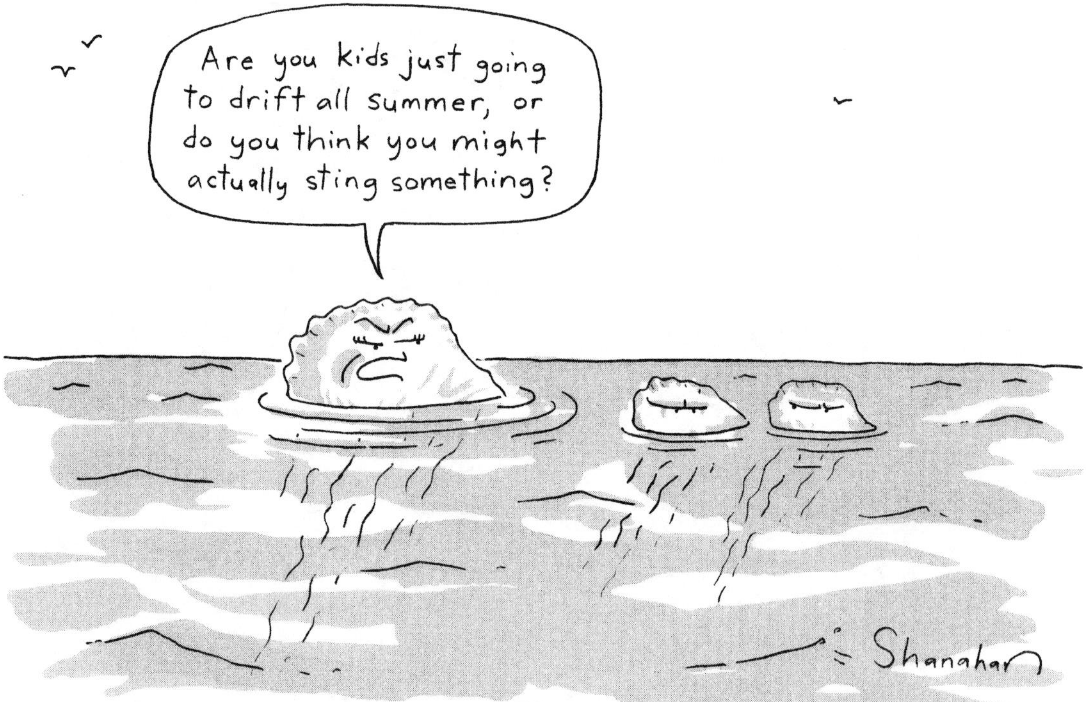
Are you kids just going to drift all summer, or do you think you might actually sting something?
Shanahan

PORTUGUESE MOM OF WAR

"Mommy wants you to know where your food comes from."

"Act your birth order!"

"Mrs. Hammond! I'd know you anywhere from little Billy's portrait of you."

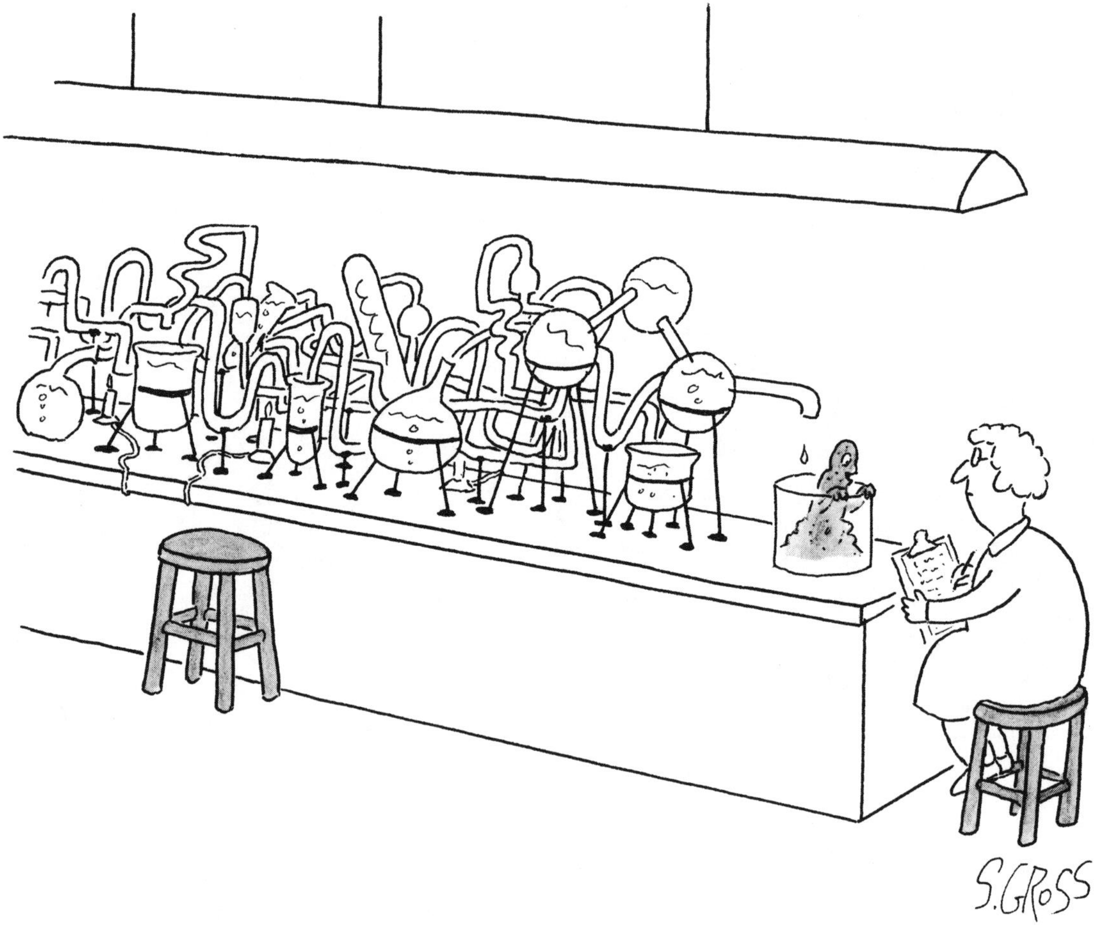
S.GROSS

"Are you my mommy?"

"I've already told Mom about my day—ask her."

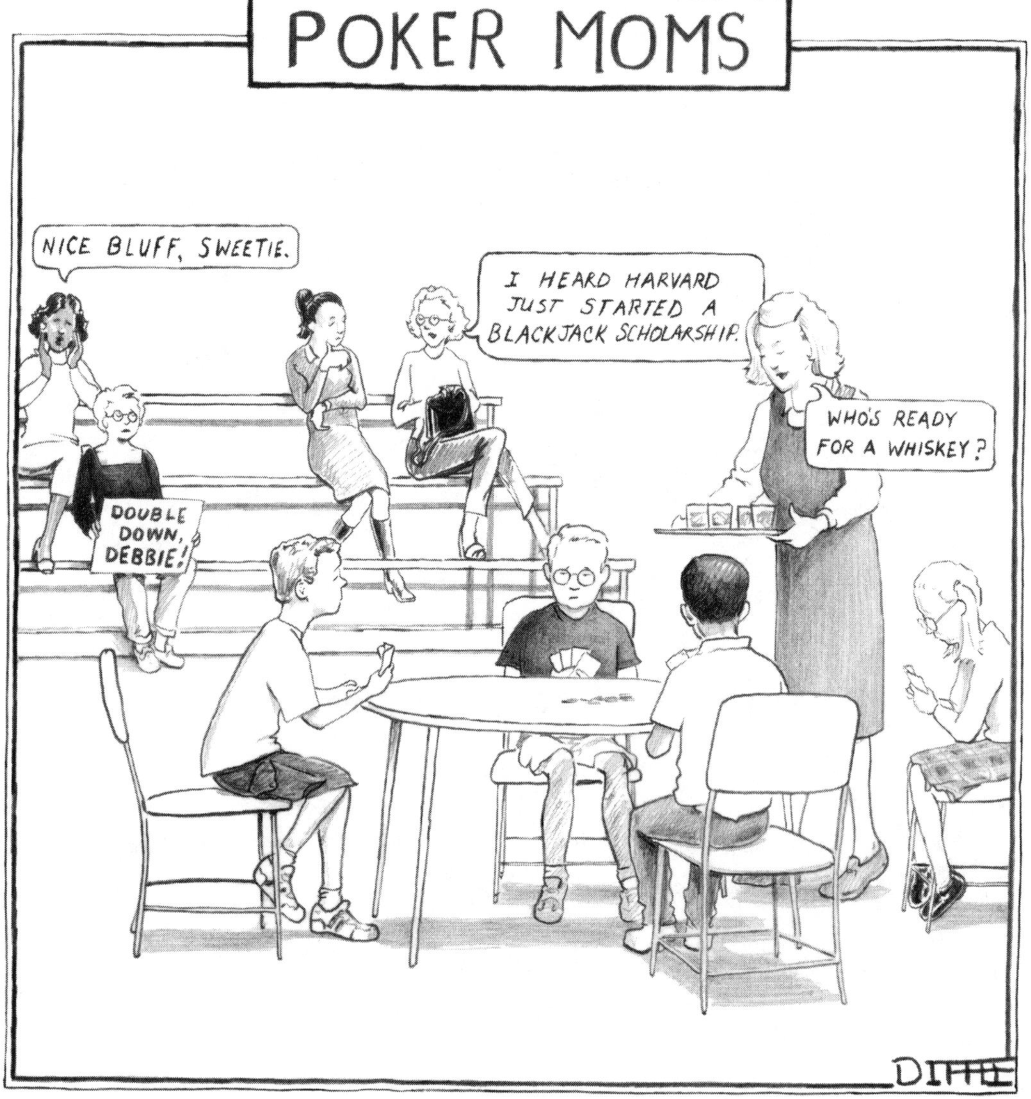
POKER MOMS
NICE BLUFF, SWEETIE.
DOUBLE DOWN, DEBBIE!
I HEARD HARVARD JUST STARTED A BLACKJACK SCHOLARSHIP.
WHO'S READY FOR A WHISKEY?

"I'm tired of the Mom channel. Switch to the Dad channel."

"*Happy Mother's Day, Mom. And ditto for
Thanksgiving and Christmas.*"

INDEX OF ARTISTS

To purchase custom cartoon books, framed prints of cartoons and covers,
or to license cartoons for use in periodicals, Web sites, or other media, please contact:

The Cartoon Bank
A *New Yorker Magazine* Company
800-897-8666 or 914-478-5604
custombooks@cartoonbank.com